U.S. Citizenship Test
Spanish • English • Español • Inglés
100 Bilingual Questions and Answers
100 Preguntas y Respuestas del Exámen de Ciudadanía de EE.UU.

U.S. Citizenship Test
(Spanish • English • Español • Inglés)
100 Bilingual Questions and Answers
100 Preguntas y Respuestas del Exámen de Ciudadania de EE.UU.

ISBN: 978-1-936583-07-2
Library of Congress Control Number: 2011932512

1. Citizenship, United States, America, U.S. 2. naturalization, citizenship 3. immigration, citizenship test, new test
4. Spanish – language   5. English – second language
6. United States – civics, government 7. United States – USCIS new test October 2008
I. Citizenship, American   II. Title
Printed in the United States of America

U.S. Citizenship Test
Spanish • English • Español • Inglés
100 Bilingual Questions and Answers

100 Preguntas y Respuestas del Exámen de Ciudadanía de EE.UU.

J.S. Aaron

Available Online:

Translation Software:

www.googletranslate.com
www.babelfish.com

(These can be helpful, but they do not give perfect translations. They are best used with single words or simple sentences.)

Also, you can see a USCIS
Sample Citizenship Interview online at:

www.welcomeesl.com
Welcome ESL
or
www.uscis.gov
United States Citizenship and Immigration Services

Also Available from Lakewood Publishing

*Learn About the United States: Quick Civics Lessons for the New NaturalizationTest
ISBN: 978-1-936583-01-0 (hardback)
ISBN: 978-0-9793538-1-9 (paperback)
ISBN 978-0-9793538-9-5 (digital/ebook)

*U.S. Citizenship Test Practice (2011-2012): How to Prepare for the United States Citizenship Test and Interview—and Pass
ISBN: 978-1-936583-14-0

U.S. Citizenship Test Questions (Multilingual) in English, Spanish, Chinese, Tagalog and Vietnamese
English -Español - 中英 - Tagalog - tiếng Việt
ISBN: 978-1-936583-11-9 (hardback)
ISBN: 978-1-936583-10-2 (paperback)

*U.S. Citizenship Test (English edition): 100 Questions and Answers Includes a Flash Card Format for Easy Practice
ISBN: 978-1-936583-04-1

*U.S.Citizenship Test (English and Spanish - Español y Inglés) 100 Bilingual Questions and Answers 100 Preguntas y respuestas del exámen de ciudadanía de EE.UU. (2011-2012)
ISBN: 978-1-936583-07-2

US Citizenship Test (Chinese-English-中英) 100 Bilingual Questions and Answers
新版公民入籍歸化考試的100道考題與答案
ISBN: 978-1-936583-05-8

U.S. Citizenship Test: 100 Bilingual Questions and Answers (Filipino – Tagalog – Ingles – English) 100 Katanungan at Sagot para sa Iksamen sa U.S. Naturalisasyon
ISBN: : 978-1-936583-09-6

U.S. Citizenship Test: 100 Bilingual Questions and Answers (Vietnamese - English - tiếng Việt - tiếng Anh) 100 câu hỏi và câu trả lời để chuẩn bị cho kỹ thi quốc tịch Mỹ
ISBN: 978-0-936583-12-6

Tabla De Contenido / Table of Contents

Español

English

Introducción
(USCIS-INS)

100 Preguntas de civismo para el Examen de E.U. Ciudadanía - Naturalización rediseñado

Las 100 preguntas y respuestas de cívica (historia y sistema de gobierno) del examen de naturalización rediseñado se encuentran a continuación. Los solicitantes que presenten la solicitud Application for Naturalization (Solicitud de naturalización), Formulario N-400 , el 1 de octubre de 2008 o después de esa fecha, deberán estudiar esta lista.

En el examen de cívica, el cual es oral, un oficial del USCIS le preguntará al solicitante hasta 10 preguntas de las 100 preguntas de cívica. El solicitante debe responder un mínimo de seis preguntas correctas para pasar satisfact-oriamente la parte de cívica del examen de naturalización.

Si bien el USCIS reconoce que podría haber otras posibles respuestas correctas a las 100 preguntas de cívica, se les insta a los solicitantes a que respondan a tales preguntas utilizando las respuestas que se proporcionan a continuación.

* Si usted tiene 65 de edad o más y hace 20 años o más que es residente permanente legal de los Estados Unidos, puede limitarse sólo al estudio de las preguntas marcadas con asterisco.

100 Preguntas de Civismo
Gobierno Americano

A: Principios de la democracia americana

1. ¿Cuál es la ley suprema de la nación?
   la Constitución

2. ¿Qué hace la Constitución?
   - establece el gobierno
   - define el gobierno
   - protege los derechos básicos de los
     ciudadanos

3. Las primeras tres palabras de la Constitución
contienen la idea de la autodeterminación (de que
el pueblo se gobierna a sí mismo). ¿Cuáles son
estas palabras?

   Nosotros el Pueblo

4. ¿Qué es una enmienda?
   - un cambio (a la Constitución)
   - una adición (a la Constitución)

5. ¿Con qué nombre se conocen las primeras diez
enmiendas a la Constitución?

   la Carta de Derechos

6. ¿Cuál es un derecho o libertad que la Primera Enmienda garantiza?*
   - expresión
   - religión
   - reunión
   - prensa
   - peticionar al gobierno

7. ¿Cuántas enmiendas tiene la Constitución?

veintisiete (27)

8. ¿Qué hizo la Declaración de Independencia?

nunció nuestra independencia (de Gran Bretaña)
declaró nuestra independencia (de Gran Bretaña)
dijo que los Estados Unidos se independizó (de
    Gran Bretaña)

9. ¿Cuáles son dos derechos en la Declaración de la Independencia?
   - la vida
   - la libertad
   - la búsqueda de la felicidad

10. ¿En qué consiste la libertad de religión?

Se puede practicar cualquier religión o no tener ninguna.

11. ¿Cuál es el sistema económico de los Estados Unidos?*
- economía capitalista
- economía del mercado

12. ¿En qué consiste el "estado de derecho" (ley y orden)?
- Todos deben obedecer la ley.
- Los líderes deben obedecer la ley.
- El gobierno debe obedecer la ley.
- Nadie está por encima de la ley.

B: Sistema de gobierno

13. Nombre una rama o parte del gobierno.*
- Congreso
- Poder legislativo
- Presidente
- Poder ejecutivo
- los tribunales
- Poder judicial

14. ¿Qué es lo que hace que una rama del gobierno no se vuelva demasiado poderosa?
- pesos y contrapesos
- separación de poderes

15. ¿Quién está a cargo de la rama ejecutiva?

el Presidente

16. ¿Quién crea las leyes federales?
- el Congreso
- el Senado y la Cámara (de Representantes)
- la legislatura (nacional o de los Estados Unidos)

17. ¿Cuáles son las dos partes que integran el Congreso de los Estados Unidos?*

el Senado y la Cámara (de Representantes)

18. ¿Cuántos senadores de los Estados Unidos hay?
cien (100)

19. ¿De cuántos años es el término de elección de un senador de los Estados Unidos?

seis (6)

20. Nombre a uno de los senadores actuales del estado donde usted vive.*

Las respuestas variarán.
[Los residentes del lDistrito de Columbia y los territorios de los   Estados Unidos deberán contestar que el D.C. (o territorio en donde vive el solicitante) no cuenta con Senadores a nivel nacional.]

21. ¿Cuántos miembros votantes tiene la Cámara de Representantes?

cuatrocientos treinta y cinco (435)

22. ¿De cuántos años es el término de elección de un representante de los Estados Unidos?

dos (2)

23. Dé el nombre de su representante a nivel nacional.
Las respuestas variarán.

[Los residentes de territorios con delegados no votantes o los comisionados residentes pueden decir el nombre de dicho delegado o comisionado. Una respuesta que indica que el territorio no tiene representantes votantes en el Congreso también es aceptable.]

24. ¿A quiénes representa un senador de los Estados Unidos?

todas las personas del estado

25. ¿Por qué tienen algunos estados más representantes que otros?
- (debido a) la población del estado
- (debido a que) tienen más gente
- (debido a que) algunos estados tienen más gente

26. ¿De cuántos años es el término de elección de un presidente?

cuatro (4)

27. ¿En qué mes votamos por un nuevo presidente?*

Noviembre

28. ¿Cómo se llama el actual Presidente de los Estados Unidos?*
- Barack Obama
- Obama

29. ¿Cómo se llama el actual Vicepresidente de los Estados Unidos?
- Joseph R. Biden, Jr.
- Joe Biden
- Biden

30. Si el Presidente ya no puede cumplir sus funciones, ¿quién se vuelve Presidente?

el Vicepresidente

31. Si tanto el Presidente como el Vicepresidente ya no pueden cumplir sus funciones, ¿quién se vuelve Presidente?

el Presidente de la Cámara de Representantes

32. ¿Quién es el Comandante en Jefe de las Fuerzas Armadas?

el Presidente

33. ¿Quién firma los proyectos de   ley para convertirlos en ley?

el Presidente

34. ¿Quién veta los proyectos de ley?

el Presidente

35. ¿Qué hace el Gabinete del Presidente?

asesora al Presidente

36. ¿Cuáles son dos puestos a nivel de gabinete?

Procurador General
Vicepresidente
Secretario de Agricultura
Secretario de Comercio
Secretario de Defensa
Secretario de Educación
Secretario de Energía
Secretario de Salud y Servicios Humanos
Secretario de Seguridad Nacional
Secretario de Vivienda y Desarrollo Urbano
Secretario del Interior
Secretario del Trabajo
Secretario de Estado
Secretario de Transporte
Secretario del Tesoro

37. ¿Qué hace la rama judicial?
   - revisa las leyes
   - explica las leyes
   - resuelve disputas (desacuerdos)
   - decide si una ley va en contra de la
      Constitución

38. ¿Cuál es el tribunal más alto de los Estados Unidos?
   la Corte Suprema de Justicia

39. ¿Cuántos jueces hay en la Corte Suprema de Justicia?
   nueve (9)

40. ¿Quién es el Presidente actual de la Corte Suprema de Justicia de los Estados Unidos?
   - John Roberts
   - John G. Roberts, Jr.)

41. De acuerdo a nuestra Constitución, algunos poderes pertenecen al gobierno federal. ¿Cuál es un poder del gobierno federal?
   - imprimir dinero
   - declarar la guerra
   - crear un ejército
   - suscribir tratados

42.   De acuerdo a nuestra Constitución, algunos poderes pertenecen a los estados. ¿Cuál es un poder de los estados?

- proveer escuelas y educación
- proveer protección (policía)
- proveer seguridad (cuerpos de bomberos)
- conceder licencias de conducir
- aprobar la zonificación y uso de la tierra

43. ¿Quién es el gobernador actual de su estado?

Las respuestas variarán.

[Los residentes del Distrito de Columbia deben decir "no tenemos gobernador".]

44. ¿Cuál es la capital de su estado?*

Las respuestas variarán.

[Los residentes del Distrito de Columbia deben contestar que el D.C. no es estado y que no tiene capital. Los residentes de los territorios de los Estados Unidos deben dar el nombre de la capital del territorio.]

45. ¿Cuáles son los dos principales partidos políticos de los Estados Unidos?*

Demócrata y Republicano

46. ¿Cuál es el partido político del Presidente actual?

(Partido) Demócrata

47. ¿Cómo se llama el Presidente actual de la Cámara de Representantes?

(Nancy) Pelosi

48. Existen cuatro enmiendas a la Constitución sobre quién puede votar. Describa una de ellas.

Ciudadanos de dieciocho (18) años en adelante (pueden votar). No se exige pagar un impuesto para votar (el impuesto para acudir a las urnas o "poll tax" en inglés). Cualquier ciudadano puede votar. (Tanto las mujeres como los hombres pueden votar.)Un hombre ciudadano de cualquier raza (puede votar).

49. ¿Cuál es una responsabilidad que corresponde sólo a los ciudadanos de los Estados Unidos?*

- prestar servicio en un jurado
- votar en una elección federal

50. ¿Cuál es un derecho que pueden ejercer sólo los ciudadanos de los Estados Unidos?

- votar en una elección federal
- postularse a un cargo político federal

51. ¿Cuáles son dos derechos que pueden ejercer todas las personas que viven en los Estados Unidos?
- libertad de expresión
- libertad de la palabra
- libertad de reunión
- libertad para peticionar al gobierno
- libertad de culto
- el derecho a portar armas

52. ¿Ante qué demostramos nuestra lealtad cuando decimos el Juramento de Lealtad (Pledge of Alle giance)?
- los Estados Unidos
- la bandera

53. ¿Cuál es una promesa que usted hace cuando se convierte en ciudadano de los Estados Unidos?
- Renunciar a la lealtad a otros países;
- defender la Constitución y las leyes de los Estados Unidos;
- obedecer las leyes de los Estados Unidos ;
- prestar servicio en las Fuerzas Armadas de los Estados Unidos (de ser necesario);
- prestar servicio a (realizar trabajo importante para) la nación (de ser necesario); ser leal a los Estados Unidos.

54. ¿Cuántos años tienen que tener los ciudadanos para votar por el Presidente?*
dieciocho (18) años en adelante

55. ¿Cuáles son dos maneras mediante las cuales los ciudadanos americanos pueden participar en su democracia?
- votar
- afiliarse a un partido político
- ayudar en una campaña
- unirse a un grupo cívico
- unirse a un grupo comunitario
- presentar su opinión sobre un asunto a un oficial elegido
- llamar a los senadores y representantes
- apoyar u oponerse públicamente a un asunto política
- postularse a un cargo político
- enviar una carta o mensaje a un periódico

56. ¿Cuál es la fecha límite para enviar la declaración federal de impuesto sobre el ingreso?*
- el 15 de abril

57. ¿Cuándo deben inscribirse todos los hombres en el Servicio Selectivo?
- a la edad de dieciocho (18) años
- entre los dieciocho (18) y veintiséis (26) años de edad

el servicio selectivo

Historia Americana

A: Época colonial e independencia

58. ¿Cuál es una razón por la que los colonos vinieron a los Estados Unidos?
- libertad
- libertad política
- libertad religiosa
- oportunidad económica
- para practicar su religión
- para huir de la persecución

59. ¿Quiénes vivían en los Estados Unidos antes de la llegada de los europeos?
- Indios americanos
- Nativos americanos

60. ¿Qué pueblo fue traído a los Estados Unidos y vendido como esclavos?
- Africanos
- gente de África

61. ¿Por qué lucharon los colonos contra los británicos?
- debido a los impuestos altos (impuestos sin representación)
- el ejército británico se quedó en sus casas (alojamiento, acuartelamiento)
- no tenían autodeterminación

62. ¿Quién escribió la Declaración de Independencia?

(Thomas) Jefferson

63. ¿Cuándo fue adoptada la Declaración de Independencia?

el 4 de julio de 1776

64. Había 13 estados originales. Nombre tres.

Carolina del Norte	Nueva Hampshire
Carolina del Sur	Nueva Jersey
Connecticut	Nu eva York
Delaware	Pennsylvania
Georgia	Rhode Island
Maryland	Virginia
Massachusetts	

65. ¿Qué ocurrió en la Convención Constitucional?

- Se redactó la Constitución.
- Los Padres Fundadores redactaron la

66. ¿Cuándo fue escrita la Constitución?

1787

67. Los ensayos conocidos como "Los Federalistas" respaldaron la aprobación de la Constitución de los Estados Unidos. Nombre uno de los autores.

- (James) Madison
- (Alexander) Hamilton
- (John) Jay
- Publius

68. Mencione una razón por la que es famoso Benjamin Franklin.

- diplomático americano
- el miembro de mayor edad de la Convención Constitucional
- primer Director General de Correos de los Estados Unidos
- autor de "Poor Richard's Almanac" (Almanaque del Pobre Richard)
- fundó las primeras bibliotecas gratuitas

69. ¿Quién se conoce como el "Padre de Nuestra Nación"?

(George) Washington

70. ¿Quién fue el primer Presidente?*
(George) Washington

George Washington,
el primer Presidente de los Estados Unidos

B: Los años 1800

71. ¿Qué territorio compró los Estados Unidos de Francia en 1803?
- el territorio de Louisiana
- Louisiana

72. Mencione una guerra durante los años 1800 en la que peleó los Estados Unidos.
- la Guerra de 1812
- la Guerra entre México y los Estados Unidos
- la Guerra Civil
- la Guerra Hispanoamericana

73. Dé el nombre de la guerra entre el Norte y el Sur de los Estados Unidos.
- la Guerra Civil
- la Guerra entre los Estados

74. Mencione un problema que condujo a la Guerra Civil.
- esclavitud
- razones económicas
- derechos de los estados

75. ¿Qué fue una cosa importante que hizo Abraham Lincoln?*
- liberó a los esclavos (Proclamación de la Emancipación)
- salvó (o preservó) la Unión
- presidió los Estados Unidos durante la Guerra Civil

Abraham Lincoln

76. ¿Qué hizo la Proclamación de la Emancipación?
- liberó a los esclavos
- liberó a los esclavos de la Confederación
- liberó a los esclavos en los estados de la Confederación
- liberó a los esclavos en la mayoría de los estados del Sur

77. ¿Qué hizo Susan B. Anthony?
- luchó por los derechos de la mujer
- luchó por los derechos civiles

C: Historia americana reciente y otra información histórica importante

78. Mencione una guerra durante los años 1900 en la que peleó los Estados Unidos.*
- la Primera Guerra Mundial
- la Segunda Guerra Mundial
- la Guerra de Corea
- la Guerra de Vietnam
- la Guerra del Golfo (Persa)

79. ¿Quién era presidente durante la Primera Guerra Mundial?

(Woodrow) Wilson

80. ¿Quién era presidente durante la Gran Depresión y la Segunda Guerra Mundial?

(Franklin) Roosevelt

81. ¿Contra qué países peleó los Estados Unidos en la Segunda Guerra Mundial?

Japón, Alemania e Italia

82. Antes de ser presidente, Eisenhower era general. ¿En qué guerra participó?

Segunda Guerra Mundial

83. Durante la Guerra Fría, ¿cuál era la principal preocupación de los Estados Unidos?

Comunismo

84. ¿Qué movimiento trató de poner fina la discriminación racial?

(el movimiento en pro de los) derechos civiles

85. ¿Qué hizo Martin Luther King, Jr.?*

- luchó por los derechos civiles
- trabajó por la igualdad de todos los ciudadanos americanos

86. ¿Qué suceso de gran magnitud ocurrió el 11 de septiembre de 2001 en los Estados Unidos?

Los terroristas atacaron los Estados Unidos.

87. Mencione una tribu de indios americanos de los Estados Unidos.

[A los oficiales del USCIS se les dará una lista de tribus amerindias reconocidas a nivel federal.]

Apache	Inuit
Arawak	Iroquois
Blackfeet	Lakota
Cherokee	Mohegan
Cheyenne	Navajo
Chippewa	Oneida
Choctaw	Pueblo
Creek	Seminole
Crow	Shawnee
Hopi	Sioux
Huron	Teton

Civismo Integrado

A: Geografía

88. Mencione uno de los dos ríos más largos en los Estados Unidos.

- (el río) Missouri
- (el río) Mississippi

89. ¿Qué océano está en la costa oeste de los Estados Unidos?

(el océano) Pacífico

90. ¿Qué océano está en la costa este de los Estados Unidos?

(el océano) Atlántico

91. Dé el nombre de un territorio de los Estados Unidos.

- Puerto Rico
- Islas Vírgenes de los Estados Unidos
- Samoa Americana
- Islas Marianas del Norte
- Guam

92. Mencione un estado que tiene frontera con Canadá.

Alaska	Nueva York (New York)
Idaho	Dakota del Norte (N. Dakota)
Maine	Ohio
Michigan	Pennsylvania
Minnesota	Vermont
Montana	Washington
Nueva Hampshire	(New Hampshire)

93. Mencione un estado que tiene frontera con México.

- Arizona
- California
- Nuevo México
- Texas

94. ¿Cuál es la capital de los Estados Unidos?*

Washington, D.C.

95. ¿Dónde está la Estatua de la Libertad?*

(el puerto de) Nueva York, Liberty Island
[Otras respuestas aceptables son Nueva Jersey, cerca de la Ciudad de Nueva York y (el río) Hudson.]

B: Símbolos

96. ¿Por qué hay 13 franjas en la bandera?

- porque representan las 13 colonias originales
- porque las franjas representan las colonias originales

97. ¿Por qué hay 50 estrellas en la bandera?*

-porque hay una estrella por cada estado
-porque cada estrella representa un estado
-porque hay 50 estados

98. ¿Cómo se llama el himno nacional?

The Star-Spangled Banner

C: Días feriados

99. ¿Cuándo celebramos el Día de la Independencia?*

el 4 de julio

100. Mencione dos días feriados nacionales de los Estados Unidos.

-el Día de Año Nuevo
-el Día de Martin Luther King, Jr.
-el Día de los Presidentes
-el Día de la Recordación
-el Día de la Independencia
-el Día del Trabajo
-el Día de la Raza (Cristóbal Colón)
-el Día de los Veteranos
-el Día de Acción de Gracias
-el Día de Navidad

el Día de la Independencia

65/20

20 Preguntas si usted tiene 65 de edad o más

65/20

Si usted tiene 65 de edad o más y hace 20 años o más que es residente permanente legal de los Estados Unidos, puede limitarse sólo al estudio de las preguntas marcadas con asterisco.

Preguntas: #6, 11, 13, 17, 20, 27, 28, 44, 45, 49, 54, 56, 70, 75, 78, 85, 94, 95, 97, 99

6. ¿Cuál es un derecho o libertad que la Primera Enmienda garantiza?*
    - expresión
    - religión
    - reunión
    - prensa
    - peticionar al gobierno

11. ¿Cuál es el sistema económico de los Estados Unidos?*
    - economía capitalista
    - economía del mercado

13. Nombre una rama o parte del gobierno.*
    - Congreso
    - Poder legislativo
    - Presidente
    - Poder ejecutivo
    - los tribunales
    - Poder judicial

17. ¿Cuáles son las dos partes que integran el Congreso de los Estados Unidos?*

el Senado y la Cámara (de Representantes)

20. Nombre a uno de los senadores actuales del estado donde usted vive.*

Las respuestas variarán.

[Los residentes del Distrito de Columbia y los territorios de los Estados Unidos deberán contestar que el D.C. (o territorio en donde vive el solicitante) no cuenta con Senadores a nivel nacional.]

27. ¿En qué mes votamos por un nuevo presidente?*

Noviembre

28. ¿Cómo se llama el actual Presidente de los Estados Unidos?*

-Barack Obama

-Obama

44. ¿Cuál es la capital de su estado?*

Las respuestas variarán.

[Los residentes del Distrito de Columbia deben contestar que el D.C. no es estado y que no tiene capital. Los residentes de los territorios de los Estados Unidos deben dar el nombre de la capital del territorio.]

45. ¿Cuáles son los dos principales partidos políticos de los Estados Unidos?*

Demócrata y Republicano

49. ¿Cuál es una responsabilidad que corresponde sólo a los ciudadanos de los Estados Unidos?*

- prestar servicio en un jurado
- votar en una elección federal

54. ¿Cuántos años tienen que tener los ciudadanos para votar por el Presidente?*

dieciocho (18) años en adelante

56. ¿Cuál es la fecha límite para enviar la declaración federal de impuesto sobre el ingreso?*

el 15 de abril

70. ¿Quién fue el primer Presidente?*

(George) Washington

75. ¿Qué fue una cosa importante que hizo Abraham Lincoln?*

- liberó a los esclavos (Proclamación de la Emancipación)
- salvó (o preservó) la Unión
- presidió los Estados Unidos durante la Guerra Civil

78. Mencione una guerra durante los años 1900 en la que peleó los Estados Unidos.*
- la Primera Guerra Mundial
- la Segunda Guerra Mundial
- la Guerra de Corea
- la Guerra de Vietnam
- la Guerra del Golfo (Persa)

85. ¿Qué hizo Martin Luther King, Jr.?*
- luchó por los derechos civiles
- trabajó por la igualdad de todos los ciudadanos americanos

94. ¿Cuál es la capital de los Estados Unidos?*
Washington, D.C.

95. ¿Dónde está la Estatua de la Libertad?*
- (el puerto de) Nueva York
- Liberty Island

[Otras respuestas aceptables son Nueva Jersey, cerca de la Ciudad de Nueva York y (el río) Hudson.]

97. ¿Por qué hay 50 estrellas en la bandera?*
- porque hay una estrella por cada estado
- porque cada estrella representa un estado
- porque hay 50 estados

99. ¿Cuándo celebramos el Día de la Independencia?*
el 4 de julio

English

100 Civics Questions and Answers for the Citizenship-Naturalization Test

Introduction

The 100 civics (history and government) questions and answers for the redesigned (new) naturalization test are listed below.

If you filed your Application for Naturalization, Form N-400, on or after October 1, 2008, you will be asked questions from this list. The civics test is an oral test and the USCIS Officer will ask you up to 10 of the 100 civics questions below.

You must answer 6 out of 10 questions correctly to pass the civics portion of the naturalization test. You will also be asked other oral questions about information on your N-400 form. Know it well.

Although USCIS knows that there may be other correct answers to the 100 civics questions below, you are encouraged to answer using the answers provided below.

Remember: Some questions will list more than one correct answer. Usually, you only need to know ONE answer.

If you need to know more than one answer, the question will tell you to know more than one answer. Otherwise, you only need to know one of the answers on the list.

Note: *If you are 65 years old or older and have been a legal permanent resident of the United States for 20 or more years, you only need to know the questions that are marked with an asterisk. (*) .

100 Civics Questions

American Government

A: Principles of American Democracy

1. What is the supreme law of the land?

   the Constitution

2. What does the Constitution do?

   - sets up the government
   - defines the government
   - protects basic rights of Americans

3. The idea of self-government is in the first three words of the Constitution. What are these words?

   We the People

4. What is an amendment?

   - a change (to the Constitution)
   - an addition (to the Constitution)

5. What do we call the first ten amendments to the Constitution?

   the Bill of Rights

6. What is one right or freedom from the First Amendment?*

- speech
- religion
- assembly
- press
- petition the government

7. How many amendments does the Constitution have?

twenty-seven (27)

8. What did the Declaration of Independence do?

- announced our independence (from Great Britain)
- declared our independence (from Great Britain)
- said that the United States is free (from Great Britain)

9. What are two rights in the Declaration of Independence?

- life
- liberty
- pursuit of happiness

10. What is freedom of religion?

You can practice any religion, or not practice (have) a religion.

11. What is the economic system in the United States?*

- capitalist economy
- market economy

12. What is the "rule of law"?

- Everyone must follow the law.
- Leaders must obey the law.
- Government must obey the law.
- No one is above the law.

B: System of Government

13. Name one branch or part of the government.*

- Congress
- legislative
- President
- executive
- the courts
- judicial

14. What stops one branch of government from becoming too powerful?

- checks and balances
- separation of powers

15. Who is in charge of the executive branch?

the President

16. Who makes federal laws?

- Congress
- Senate and House (of Representatives)
- (U.S. or national) legislature

17. What are the two parts of the U.S. Congress?*

the Senate and House (of Representatives)

18. How many U.S. Senators are there?

one hundred (100)

19. We elect a U.S. Senator for how many years?

six (6)

20. Who is one of your state's U.S. Senators now?*

▪ Answers will be different for each state. Check the internet **www.senate.gov** for the current names in your state. [District of Columbia residents and residents of U.S. territories should answer that D.C. (or the territory where the applicant lives) has no U.S. Senators.]

21. The House of Representatives has how many voting members?

four hundred thirty-five (435)

22. We elect a U.S. Representative for how many years?

two (2)

23. Name your U.S. Representative.

▪ Answers will be different for each area. See the website: www.house.gov for the newest names. [Residents of territories with non-voting Delegates or Resident Commissioners may provide the name of that Delegate or Commissioner. Also acceptable is any statement that the territory has no (voting) Representatives in Congress.]

24. Who does a U.S. Senator represent?

all people of the state

25. Why do some states have more Representatives than other states?

- (because of) the state's population
- (because) they have more people
- (because) some states have more people

26. We elect a President for how many years?

four (4)

27. In what month do we vote for President?*

November

28. What is the name of the President of the United States now?*

- Barack Obama
- Obama

29. What is the name of the Vice President of the United States now?

- Joseph R. Biden, Jr.
- Joe Biden
- Biden

30. If the President can no longer serve, who becomes President?

the Vice President

31. If both the President and the Vice President can no longer serve, who becomes President?

the Speaker of the House

32. Who is the Commander in Chief of the military?

the President

33. Who signs bills to become laws?

the President

34. Who vetoes bills?

the President

35. What does the President's Cabinet do?

advises the President

36. What are two Cabinet-level positions?

- Vice President
- Attorney General
- Secretary of Agriculture
- Secretary of Commerce
- Secretary of Defense
- Secretary of Education
- Secretary of Energy
- Secretary of Health and Human Services
- Secretary of Homeland Security
- Secretary of Housing and Urban Development
- Secretary of the Interior
- Secretary of Labor
- Secretary of State
- Secretary of Transportation
- Secretary of the Treasury
- Secretary of Veterans Affairs

37. What does the judicial branch do?

- reviews laws
- explains laws
- resolves disputes (disagreements)
- decides if a law goes against the Constitution

38. What is the highest court in the United States?

the Supreme Court

39. How many justices are on the Supreme Court?

nine (9)

40. Who is the Chief Justice of the United States now?

John Roberts (John G. Roberts, Jr.)

41. Under our Constitution, some powers belong to the federal government. What is one power of the federal government?

- to print money
- to declare war
- to create an army
- to make treaties

42. Under our Constitution, some powers belong to the states. What is one power of the states?

- provide schooling and education
- provide protection (police)
- provide safety (fire departments)
- give a driver's license
- approve zoning and land use

43. Who is the Governor of your state now?

▪ Answers will be different for each state. [District of Columbia residents should answer that D.C. does not have a Governor.]

44. What is the capital of your state?*

The States and the State Capitals

Alabama - Montgomery
Alaska - Juneau
Arizona - Phoenix
Arkansas - Little Rock
California - Sacramento
Colorado - Denver
Connecticut - Hartford
Delaware - Dover
Florida - Tallahassee
Georgia - Atlanta
Hawaii - Honolulu
Idaho - Boise
Illinois - Springfield
Indiana - Indianapolis
Iowa - Des Moines
Kansas - Topeka
Kentucky - Frankfort
Louisiana - Baton Rouge
Maine - Augusta
Maryland - Annapolis
Massachusetts - Boston
Michigan - Lansing
Minnesota - St. Paul
Mississippi - Jackson
Missouri - Jefferson City
Montana - Helena

Nebraska - Lincoln
Nevada - Carson City
New Hampshire - Concord
New Jersey - Trenton
New Mexico - Santa Fe
New York - Albany
North Carolina - Raleigh
North Dakota - Bismarck
Ohio - Columbus
Oklahoma - Oklahoma City
Oregon - Salem
Pennsylvania - Harrisburg
Rhode Island - Providence
South Carolina - Columbia
South Dakota - Pierre
Tennessee - Nashville
Texas - Austin
Utah - Salt Lake City
Vermont - Montpelier
Virginia - Richmond
Washington - Olympia
West Virginia - Charleston
Wisconsin - Madison
Wyoming - Cheyenne

[District of Columbia residents should answer that D.C. is not a state and does not have a capital. Residents of U.S. territories should name the capital of the territory.]

45. What are the two major political parties in the United States?*

Democratic and Republican

46. What is the political party of the President now?

Democratic (Party)

47. What is the name of the Speaker of the House of Representatives now?

(John) Boehner

C: Rights and Responsibilities

48. There are four amendments to the Constitution about who can vote. Describe one of them.

- Citizens eighteen (18) and older (can vote).
- You don't have to pay (a poll tax) to vote.
- Any citizen can vote. (Women and men can vote.)
- A male citizen of any race (can vote).

49. What is one responsibility that is only for United States citizens?*

(1) serve on a jury;
(2) vote in a federal election

50. Name one right only for United States citizens.

- vote in a federal election
- run for federal office

51. What are <u>two</u> rights of everyone living in the United States?

- freedom of expression
- freedom of speech
- freedom of assembly
- freedom to petition the government
- freedom of worship
- the right to bear arms

52. What do we show loyalty to when we say the Pledge of Allegiance?

- the United States
- the flag

53. What is one promise you make when you become a United States citizen?

- give up loyalty to other countries
- defend the Constitution and laws of the United States
- obey the laws of the United States
- serve in the U.S. military (if needed)
- serve (do important work for) the nation (if needed)
- be loyal to the United States

54. How old do citizens have to be to vote for President?*

- eighteen (18) and older

55. What are two ways that Americans can participate in their democracy?

- vote
- join a political party
- help with a campaign
- join a civic group
- join a community group
- give an elected official your opinion on an issue
- call Senators and Representatives
- publicly support or oppose an issue or policy
- run for office write to a newspaper

56. When is the last day you can send in federal income tax forms?*

April 15

57. When must all men register for the Selective Service?

- at age eighteen (18)
- between eighteen (18) and twenty-six (26)

American History

A: Colonial Period and Independence

58. What is one reason colonists came to America?

- freedom
- political liberty
- religious freedom
- economic opportunity
- practice their religion
- escape persecution

59. Who lived in America before the Europeans arrived?

- American Indians
- Native Americans

60. What group of people was taken to America and sold as slaves?

- Africans
- people from Africa

61. Why did the colonists fight the British?

- because of high taxes ("taxation without representation")
- because the British army stayed in their - houses (boarding, quartering)
- because they didn't have self-government

62. Who wrote the Declaration of Independence?

(Thomas) Jefferson

63. When was the Declaration of Independence adopted?

July 4, 1776

64. There were 13 original states. Name three.

Connecticut	New York
Delaware	North Carolina
Georgia	Pennsylvania
Massachusetts	Rhode Island
Maryland	South Carolina
New Hampshire	Virginia
New Jersey	

65. What happened at the Constitutional Convention?

- The Constitution was written.
- The Founding Fathers wrote the Constitution.

66. When was the Constitution written?

1787

67. The Federalist Papers supported the passage of the U.S. Constitution. Name one of the writers.

- (James) Madison
- (Alexander) Hamilton
- (John) Jay
- Publius

68. What is one thing Benjamin Franklin is famous for?

- being a U.S. diplomat
- the oldest member of the Constitutional Convention
- first Postmaster General of the United States
- writer of "Poor Richard's Almanac"
- started the first free libraries

69. Who is the "Father of Our Country"?

(George) Washington

70. Who was the first President?*

(George) Washington

B: 1800s

71. What territory did the United States buy from France in 1803?

- the Louisiana Territory
- Louisiana

72. Name one war fought by the United States in the 1800s.

- War of 1812
- Mexican-American War
- Civil War
- Spanish-American War

73. Name the U.S. war between the North and the South.

- the Civil War
- the War between the States

74. Name one problem that led to the Civil War.

- slavery
- economic reasons
- states' rights

75. What was one important thing that Abraham Lincoln did?*

- freed the slaves (Emancipation Proclamation)
- saved (or preserved) the Union
- led the United States during the Civil War

76. What did the Emancipation Proclamation do?

- freed the slaves
- freed slaves in the Confederacy
- freed slaves in the Confederate states
- freed slaves in most Southern states

77. What did Susan B. Anthony do?

- fought for women's rights
- fought for civil rights

C: Recent American History and Other Important Historical Information

78. Name one war fought by the United States in the 1900s.*

- World War I
- World War II
- Korean War
- Vietnam War
- (Persian) Gulf War

79. Who was President during World War I?

(Woodrow) Wilson

80. Who was President during the Great Depression and World War II?

(Franklin) Roosevelt

81. Who did the United States fight in World War II?

Japan, Germany, and Italy

82. Before he was President, Eisenhower was a general. What war was he in?

World War II

83. During the Cold War, what was the main concern of the United States?

Communism

84. What movement tried to end racial discrimination?

civil rights (movement)

85. What did Martin Luther King, Jr. do?*

- fought for civil rights
- worked for equality for all Americans

86. What major event happened on September 11, 2001, in the United States?

- Terrorists attacked the United States.

87. Name one American Indian tribe in the United States.

[USCIS Officers will be supplied with a list of federally recognized American Indian tribes.]

Apache	Inuit
Arawak	Iroquois
Blackfeet	Lakota
Cherokee	Mohegan
Cheyenne	Navajo
Chippewa	Oneida
Choctaw	Pueblo
Creek	Seminole
Crow	Shawnee
Hopi	Sioux
Huron	Teton

Integrated Civics

A: Geography

88. Name one of the two longest rivers in the United States.

- Missouri (River)
- Mississippi (River)

89. What ocean is on the West Coast of the United States?

Pacific (Ocean)

90. What ocean is on the East Coast of the United States?

Atlantic (Ocean)

91. Name one U.S. territory.

- Puerto Rico
- U.S. Virgin Islands
- American Samoa
- Northern Mariana Islands
- Guam

92. Name one state that borders Canada.

Alaska	New York
Idaho	North Dakota
Maine	Ohio
Michigan	Pennsylvania
Minnesota	Vermont
Montana	Washington
New Hampshire	

93. Name one state that borders Mexico.

- Arizona
- California
- New Mexico
- Texas

94. What is the capital of the United States?*

Washington, D.C.

95. Where is the Statue of Liberty?*

- New York (Harbor)
- Liberty Island

[Also correct are "New Jersey", "near New York City", and "on the Hudson (River)".]

B: Symbols

96. Why does the flag have 13 stripes?

- because there were 13 original colonies
- because the stripes represent the original colonies

97. Why does the flag have 50 stars?*

- because there is one star for each state
- because each star represents a state
- because there are 50 states

98. What is the name of the national anthem?

The Star-Spangled Banner

C: Holidays

99. When do we celebrate Independence Day?*

July 4

100. Name two national U.S. holidays.

New Year's Day

Martin Luther King, Jr. Day

Presidents' Day

Memorial Day

Independence Day

Labor Day

Columbus Day

Veterans Day

Thanksgiving

Christmas

English

65/20

*If you are 65 years old or older and have been a legal permanent resident of the United States for 20 or more years, you only need to know the questions that have been marked with an asterisk. (*)

They are also listed below.
Questions: #6, 11, 13, 17, 20, 27, 28, 44, 45, 49, 54, 56, 70, 75, 78, 85, 94, 95, 97, 99

People who are 65 years old (or older) and have been permanent residents for 20 years (or more) do not need to know all 100 questions. You only need to know the answers to the 20 questions in this section.

6. What is one right or freedom from the First Amendment?*

- speech
- religion
- assembly
- press
- petition the government

11. What is the economic system in the United States?*

- capitalist economy
- market economy

13. Name one branch or part of the government.*

- Congress (or legislative)
- President (or executive)
- the courts (or judicial)

17. What are the two parts of the U.S. Congress?*

the Senate and House (of Representatives)

20. Who is one of your state's U.S. Senators now?*

Answers will be different for each state. [District of Columbia residents and residents of U.S. territories should answer that D.C. (or the territory where the applicant lives) has no U.S. Senators.]

27. In what month do we vote for President?*

November

28. What is the name of the President of the United States now?*

- Barack Obama
- Obama

44. What is the capital of your state?*

Answers will be different by state. See page 48. [District of Columbia residents should answer that D.C. is not a state and does not have a capital. Residents of U.S. territories should name the capital of the territory.]

66

45. What are the two major political parties in the United States?*

Democratic and Republican

49. What is one responsibility that is only for United States citizens?*

- serve on a jury
- vote in a federal election
- the flag

54. How old do citizens have to be to vote for President?*

eighteen (18) and older

56. When is the last day you can send in federal income tax forms?*

April 15

70. Who was the first President?*

(George) Washington

75. What was one important thing that Abraham Lincoln did?*

- freed the slaves (Emancipation Proclamation)
- saved (or preserved) the Union
- led the United States during the Civil War

78. Name one war fought by the United States in the 1900s.*

- World War I
- World War II
- Korean War
- Vietnam War
- (Persian) Gulf War

85. What did Martin Luther King, Jr. do?*

- fought for civil rights
- worked for equality for all Americans

94. What is the capital of the United States?*

Washington, D.C.

95. Where is the Statue of Liberty?*

- New York (Harbor)
- Liberty Island

[Also acceptable are New Jersey, near New York City, and on the Hudson (River).]

97. Why does the flag have 50 stars?*

- because there is one star for each state
- because each star represents a state
- because there are 50 states

99. When do we celebrate Independence Day?*

July 4

Reading Vocabulary
(USCIS Recommended)

Reading Vocabulary (USCIS Recommended List)

Your reading test will be 1-3 sentences. You must read one (1) of three (3) sentences correctly to show that you read English. The USCIS (INS) does not tell the words they use on the reading test. These are the words the USCIS recommends as the basic vocabulary that you should know, but there may be other words to read on the test, too.

Question Words
how
what
when
where
why
who

Other
a
for
here
in
of
on
the
to
we

Verbs
can
come
do/does
elects
have/has
be/is/are/was
lives/lived
meet
name
pay
vote
want

Other (content)
colors
dollar bill
first
largest
many
most
north
one
people
second
south

People

George Washington
Abraham Lincoln

Places

America
United States
U.S.

Civics

American flag
Bill of Rights
capital
citizen
city
Congress
country
Father of Our Country
government
President
right
Senators
state/states
White House

Holidays

Presidents' Day
Memorial Day
Flag Day
Independence Day
Labor Day
Columbus Day
Thanksgiving

Writing Vocabulary
(USCIS Recommended)

Writing Vocabulary (USCIS Recommended List)

You will be read 1-3 short sentences and asked to write them. You must write one (1) out of three (3) sentences correctly. The USCIS (INS) does not tell the words they use on the writing test. These are the words they recommend as the basic vocabulary that you should know, but there may be other words to write on the test, too.

Months

February
September
May
October
June
November
July

People

Adams
Lincoln
Washington

Civics

American Indian
capital
citizens
Civil War
Congress
Father of Our Country
flag
free
freedom of speech
President
right
Senators
state/states
White House

Holidays

Presidents' Day
Columbus Day
Thanksgiving
Flag Day

Labor Day
Memorial Day
Independence Day

Places

Alaska
California
Canada
Delaware
Mexico
New York City
Washington, D.C.
United States

Verbs

be/is/was
can
come
elect
have/has
lives/lived
meets
pay
vote
want

Other (content)

blue
dollar bill
fifty / 50
first
largest
most
north
one

Other

one hundred/ 100
people
red
second
south
taxes
white

Other (Function)

and
during
for
here

of
on
the
to

For More Information

More Information - Phone, Mail, Online

Si usted no sabe a qué departamento dirigir una pregunta, llame al 1-800-FED-INFO (o al 1-800-333-4636) para averiguar dónde debe llamar. Si tiene dificultades para oír, llame al: 1-800-326-2996. También puede visitar el sitio en la web: **http://www.USA.gov** para obtener información general acerca de los departamentos y dependencias federales.

(If you don't know where to call, start with **1-800-FED-INFO** (or 1-800-333-4636) for more information. For hard-of- hearing, call 1-800-326-2996. The government also has a website: **http://www.USA.gov** for general information about government agencies.)

U.S. Citizenship and Immigration Services (USCIS)
(Servicio de Ciudadanía e Immigracion de los EE.UU.)
Teléfono: 1-800-375-5283
Si tiene dificultades para oír: 1-800-767-1833
http://www.uscis.gov

Internal Revenue Service (IRS)
(Servicio de Rentas Internas)
Teléfono: 1-800-829-1040
Si tiene dificultades para oír: 1-800-829-4059
http://www.irs.gov

U.S. Immigration and Customs Enforcement (ICE)
(Servicio de Immigracion e de Fiscalizacione de Aduanas)
http://www.ice.gov

Selective Service System (SSS)
(Sistema del Servicio Sélectivo)
Registration Information Office
PO Box 94638
Palatine, IL 60094-4638
Teléfono: 847-688-6888
Si tiene dificultades para oír: 847-688-2567
http://www.sss.gov

Social Security Administration (SSA)
(Administración de Seguro Social)
Office of Public Inquiries
6401 Security Boulevard
Baltimore, MD 21235
Teléfono: 1-800-772-1213
Si tiene dificultades para oír: 1-800-325-0778
http://www.socialsecurity.gov or
http://www.segurosocial.gov/espanol/.

Department of Homeland Security (DHS)
(Departmento de Seguridad Nacional)
U.S. Department of Homeland Security
Washington, DC 20528
http://www.dhs.gov

Department of Education (ED)
(Departmento de Educación)
U.S. Department of Education
400 Maryland Avenue SW
Washington, DC 20202
Teléfono: 1-800-872-5327
Si tiene dificultades para oír: 1-800-437-0833
http://www.ed.gov

Equal Employment Opportunity Commission (EEOC)
(Comisión de Igualidad de Oportunidades de Empleo)
U.S. Equal Employment Opportunity Commission
1801 L Street NW
Washington, DC 20507
Teléfono: 1-800-669-4000
Si tiene dificultades para oír: 1-800-669-6820
http://www.eeoc.gov

Department of Health and Human Services (HHS)
(Departmento de Salud y Servicios Humanos)
U.S. Department of Health and Human Services
200 Independence Avenue SW
Washington, DC 20201
Teléfono: 1-877-696-6775
http://www.hhs.gov

U.S. Customs and Border Protection (CBP)
(Servicio de Aduanas y Protección de Fronteras)
Teléfono: 202-354-1000
http://www.cbp.gov

Department of Housing and Urban Development (HUD)
(Departmento de Viviendo y Desarrollo Urbano)
U.S. Department of Housing and Urban Development
451 7th Street SW
Washington, DC 20410
Teléfono: 202-708-1112
Si tiene dificultades para oír: 202-708-1455
http://www.hud.gov

Department of Justice (DOJ)
(Departmento de Justicia)
U.S. Department of Justice
950 Pennsylvania Avenue NW
Washington, DC 20530-0001
Teléfono: 202-514-2000
http://www.usdoj.gov

Department of State (DOS)
(Departmento de Estado)
U.S. Department of State
2201 C Street NW
Washington, DC 20520
Teléfono: 202-647-4000
http://www.state.gov

You Can Also....

Check online:

Find new information and practice materials:

At the "Welcome ESL" website: **www.welcomeesl.com**

Visit the USCIS website at: **http://www.uscis.gov**

You can also go to: **http://www.welcometousa.gov**

Telephone:

Call Customer Service at 1-800-375-5283 or
1-800-767-1833 (hearing impaired).

To get the USCIS (INS) forms, call: 1-800-870-3676 or
look on the USCIS website: **http://www.uscis.gov**

To Remember:
Keep Records, Notes and Important Dates Here

_____

_____

_____

_____

_____

_____

_____

_____

_____

_____

_____

_____

_____

_____

_____

_____

_____

_____

_____

_____

_____

For group discounts, contact Lakewood Publishing at:
representative@lakewoodpublishing.com

Other Books in the Bilingual Citizenship Test Series

English with Flashcards

Spanish - English

Vietnamese - English

Filipino/Tagalog - English

Also from Lakewood Publishing

U.S. Citizenship
Test Questions
in
English, Spanish, Chinese, Tagalog
and Vietnamese
English   Español   中文
Tagalog   tiếng Việt

100 USCIS Civics Questions & Answers
Questions in a Flashcard Format (English)
20 Questions for People 65 and Older
USCIS Vocabulary Lists and More
J.S. Aaron

U.S. Citizenship Test Questions

includes
Civics Questions and
Answers in English,
Spanish, Chinese,
Tagalog and
Vietnamese,
Flashcards in English,
20 Questions for
Seniors ,
Contact Information
and More

Learn About the United States
Quick Civics Lessons for the New U.S. Naturalization Test

Short readings that
explain all the civics
questions on the US
citizenship test,what
they mean and why
the information is so
important for citizens
to know.

Learn About the
United States
Quick Civics Lessons
for the New Naturalization Test

U.S. Citizenship and
Immigration Service   USCIS

31292125R00058

Made in the USA
Charleston, SC
10 July 2014